NATHAN HALE

As a young boy, Nathan Hale loved to play outdoors and to read. When he grew up he became a teacher. At the same time he was a teacher, there was trouble between the American colonies and the King of England. Soon there was a war and Nathan joined the American Army. One day he said he would help General George Washington by spying on the British.

Nathan was very brave but he was captured by the British. Because he was a spy, the British were going to kill him. Just before he was to die, Nathan Hale said, "I only regret that I have but one life to lose for my country." This is the story of Nathan Hale, a man who loved his country and helped to make it free.

A SEE AND READ

Beginning to Read Biography

NATHAN
HALE

by Virginia Frances Voight

Illustrated by Frank Aloise

G. P. Putnam's Sons   New York

Other SEE AND READ
Beginning to Read Biographies

ABRAHAM LINCOLN

GEORGE WASHINGTON

POCAHONTAS

CHRISTOPHER COLUMBUS

JOHN FITZGERALD KENNEDY

DANIEL BOONE

NATHAN HALE

Text © 1965 by Virginia Frances Voight
Illustrations © 1965 by Frank Aloise
Library of Congress Catalog Card Number: 65-10872
All rights reserved
MANUFACTURED IN THE UNITED STATES OF AMERICA
Published simultaneously in the Dominion of
Canada by Longmans Canada Limited, Toronto
07209

There were ten jolly boys and girls in the Hale farmhouse. Nathan was one of the middle ones. But he was the leader when it came to doing things.

The Hales lived on a big farm with woods all around. In those days the American states were called "colonies." Nathan and his family lived in the Colony of Connecticut.

The King of England, who lived across the sea, ruled the American colonies. But to the children on the Hale farm, England and the King seemed very far away.

Everyone in the Hale family had to work hard.

The boys helped with the farm work. They took care of the sheep and milked the cows. They plowed the fields and planted Indian corn. They took the ripe corn to the mill to be ground into golden cornmeal.

The girls helped their mother with the housework. They made cream into butter in a wooden churn. They baked johnnycake of the cornmeal in the fireplace oven. Mmm. Hot johnny-cake and fresh-churned butter tasted so good at dinnertime!

The boys sheared the sheep and washed the wool. The girls spun the wool into thread at the spinning wheel. They wove the woolen thread into cloth on the big loom. They cut and sewed the cloth into clothing for all the family.

But the boys and girls on the Hale farm had fun too. Nathan loved to run and jump. No one else could run so fast or jump so far as he. On hot summer days he liked to swim in a deep hole in the brook.

In autumn Nathan and his brothers and sisters went to the woods to gather nuts. The squirrels scolded the children from the trees. But there were enough nuts for squirrels and children alike.

On Sunday the Hale family walked to the white church in the village. It gave them a good feeling to go to church together.

Nathan was an outdoor boy but he loved to read as well as play. He liked school and when he later finished college, he became a teacher.

Nathan's first school was a tiny red house on the bank of the Connecticut River. On pleasant days he took his classes for long walks in the woods. They learned the ways of wild animals and birds. They learned the names of flowers and trees.

When Nathan went away to teach
at another school, the children missed
him very much.

But Nathan was not to stay a teacher for long. For now there was trouble between the American colonies and the King of England. The King needed money. He hoped to get some by making the American people pay him taxes.

One thing that he taxed was tea.
This meant that the people must pay
the King money every time they
bought tea. The people refused to pay
the tax. The King, they said, had no
right to this money.

The King grew very angry. He sent soldiers to the colonies to force the Americans to obey him. By this time the Americans were angry also. They reminded the King that they were a free people. And they would fight for their freedom if they had to!

Everywhere in the colonies people made ready for the coming of the King's red-coated soldiers.

American farmers and schoolteachers, storekeepers and lawyers, began training to be soldiers themselves. Nathan Hale trained with the other young men of his town. No one wanted war. But the Connecticut men had to be ready to fight the redcoats if they came.

One day a rider rushed into the town where Nathan was teaching school.

He brought exciting news from the Colony of Massachusetts. In Massachusetts some American farmers had fought a battle with the King's soldiers.

The farmers had made the redcoats run! Now they had the King's
army shut up in Boston. They needed
help to drive the redcoats out of the
town and away. They asked their
neighbors in Connecticut and the
other colonies to come and help.

Nathan was one of the first to take his gun and go to Massachusetts.

Men came also from the other colonies. Now the colonies had an army of their own to fight the King's men.

A tall soldier named George Washington was made general of the new army.

Before long General Washington and his army chased the King's soldiers out of Massachusetts. Then the general moved the army to New York in a great hurry. The King's ships, he had learned, were sailing to New York. The American Army had to go there too.

The Americans made camp in New York. There they heard more news.

While they were fighting the red-coats, other men from all the colonies had met in Philadelphia. This meeting of men was called a Congress. The Congress made laws and raised money to carry on the war. Now the men in

Congress had agreed to free themselves from the King forever. They
signed a paper which was called the
Declaration of Independence. In this
paper Congress declared the colonies
to be free and independent states.

Together, the colonies took on a
new name, the United States of
America!

Nathan Hale was excited and happy to be living in a new country. The United States of America — How fine it sounded! Nathan loved his new country. He was proud to be helping General Washington win freedom for the United States.

Then one day the Americans at
New York saw a great many tall ships
out on the water. The ships were
crowded with the red-coated soldiers
of the King. The King had many more
soldiers than General Washington.

The King's men had better guns and bigger cannon than the Americans.

General Washington's army and the King's army fought a battle on Long Island. This time the King's army won. The Americans moved back, but they were ready to fight again.

General Washington had to know what the King's general would do next. He asked that some soldier go back to Long Island to spy upon the redcoats.

The spy had to find out how many soldiers there were in the King's army. He had to find out how many cannon and guns they had. This would help General Washington make ready for the next battle.

None of the soldiers wanted to be a spy. A spy must pretend not to be a soldier. He must hide in the redcoat camp to watch and listen. If the redcoats caught him, he would die far from his own people.

At last Nathan Hale said he would go to Long Island for General Washington.

"I will be a spy to help my country," he said.

Nathan put on an old coat and hat.
He left his pistols with a friend. He
asked Captain Pond, a sailor, to take
him to Long Island in his boat.

They started out after dark. Many
of the King's ships were sailing up and
down, looking for American ships.
But at last they came safely to Long
Island. There, as the sun came up,
Captain Pond left Nathan on a lonely
beach.

"I will come back for you in three days," said the captain.

"I will be here," Nathan told him.

Captain Pond sailed away. Nathan watched the boat grow smaller and smaller. Soon he could not see it at all. Now he was alone and far from his friends.

Nathan crossed the beach and climbed a sandy hill. Then he walked through some fields to the road. No one saw him. No one knew that an American spy had come to Long Island.

As he walked along the road, he met
a red-coated soldier of the King.

The redcoat pulled up his horse.
"Who are you?" he asked Nathan.

"I am a teacher," said Nathan.

The redcoat looked as if he did not
believe Nathan, but he rode away.

Nathan was a little afraid. What if the redcoat should bring other soldiers to take him prisoner? Then he made himself walk on with a quick step. He must do his work for General Washington. He must not be afraid.

Nathan walked miles and miles that day. He saw that there were many redcoats on Long Island. The King had a very large army.

That night Nathan slept in a field beside the road. The crickets were singing all around. Their voices made him think of home. In the dark sky bright stars were twinkling.

"Those same stars are twinkling above our farm," thought Nathan. "And above my friends in the army."

The thought made him feel less alone.

The next morning Nathan washed his face at a little spring beside the road. A friendly woman at a farm gave him some bread and butter. Nathan took to the road again. He ate the good bread as he walked with long steps.

Soon he came to the big camp of the King's soldiers. He walked around and looked at everything. He talked to the redcoats and looked at their guns. He saw the King's big cannon.

He listened to the talk of the King's
men. He wrote down everything he
thought General Washington would
want to know. He drew pictures of
the guns. Then he hid the papers in
his shoe.

Suddenly Nathan heard the sound of cannon booming across the water from New York. BOOM BOOM BOOM. The Americans and the King's men were fighting again. It was time for him to go back to his own army.

That night he slept under some pine trees in a wood. In the morning he started back to the beach where he was to meet Captain Pond. It was a long, long walk. At noon he cut wood at a farmhouse to pay for his dinner.

Back on the road again, he met the
same red-coated rider. The redcoat
gave him a hard look but did not say
anything. Nathan walked on quickly.
At a turn in the road, he looked back.
The redcoat was still sitting there on
his horse.

"He is watching me," Nathan thought.

Had the redcoat guessed that he was a spy? The thought made him walk faster than ever.

He walked all night. At sunup he was waiting on the beach. He waited and waited. The boat did not come. Maybe the King's ships were keeping Captain Pond away from Long Island!

Nathan could not let the King's men see him waiting near the water. He had to find a place to hide until Captain Pond came for him. He climbed the hill and started back across the fields.

Then he saw a man on a horse. It was the redcoat! Nathan knew the man had followed him. Now he was really afraid.

Nathan ran back across the field and down the sandy hill. Oh, if only Captain Pond would come!

"Stop in the name of the King!"
shouted the redcoat.

He galloped to the top of the hill.
He jumped off his horse and ran down
to the beach. He pulled out his pistol
and called to Nathan to stop.

Nathan had no pistol. He looked
around. There was no place on the
beach to hide!

Suddenly he gave a happy cry.

Out on the water, a boat had come around some rocks. Nathan thought it was Captain Pond's boat. He called to the sailors to hurry. He ran down to the water. Then he stopped short.

The boat was close to the beach now. Nathan saw that the men on board were sailors of the King.

Nathan turned to run. The redcoat with the pistol was standing right behind him!

The redcoat pointed the pistol. "You are my prisoner!" he cried.

Now the sailors were jumping from the boat to the sand. They ran to where Nathan stood with the redcoat.

"This man is a spy," the redcoat told them.

The sailors looked at Nathan. "Are you an American?" one of them asked him.

"Yes," Nathan said proudly. "I am Captain Nathan Hale of the American Army."

He was glad not to have to pretend any longer.

The sailors looked in Nathan's coat. They looked in his hat. At last they found the papers in his shoe.

"Now we know that you really are a spy," they told him.

They put him on the boat and took him to the King's general.

The King's general read Nathan's papers with care. He looked at the pictures of the guns. These things told him that the prisoner was a very bright young man.

"Why did you come here to spy on us?" asked the general.

"I wanted to help win freedom for my country," said Nathan.

He stood tall and straight. His eyes were bright. He did not look afraid. The King's general liked Nathan's good looks.

"The King can use good soldiers like you," said the general. "If you will come in with us, I will make you a captain of the King's men. I will give you more money than you get in the American Army."

Nathan was angry because the general had asked him to leave his own people.

"I love my own country," he said. "I will not fight for the King."

"Then tomorrow you must die," said the general.

The King's soldiers took Nathan to prison. The next morning they brought him out into the prison yard. Drums beat with a sad roll.

Many redcoats had come to see the spy hang. Some were sorry for him. All of them thought that he looked like a brave young soldier.

Nathan stood straight and proud. He had said his prayers. Now he would not let the redcoats think that he was afraid.

"Well, Mr. Spy," said a redcoat, "you are going to die. Now are you sorry that you fought against the King?"

"No," said Nathan.

His voice rang out so that every one of the King's men could hear.

"I only regret that I have but one life to lose for my country."

All this happened a long time ago, but Nathan Hale's brave words still live for us. They help us remember Nathan as a boy who loved his country.

He was one of those who died so
that all Americans can be free.

KEY WORDS

army	declared	pretend
battle	force	prisoner (prison)
beach	free (freedom)	regret
cannon	general	sailing (sailed)
chase	gun	scolded
churn	hang	soldiers
college	independent	shear
colony (ies)	johnnycake	spinning wheel
Congress	law (laws)	spy
Connecticut	Long Island	tax
crickets	loom	twinkling
Declaration of	Massachusetts	United States
Independence	New York	wool
die (died)	pistol (s)	

The Author

VIRGINIA FRANCES VOIGHT's storybooks and nature tales have been delighting young readers in the United States and Europe for many years. She has published some ten children's books in addition to numerous stories and articles in BOY'S LIFE, TRAILS FOR JUNIORS, AMERICAN GIRL, and other periodicals for children.

A lifelong student of American history, Miss Voight also maintains an active interest in the conservation of wildlife and natural resources. She makes her home in Connecticut and spends her summers in Maine, gathering material for the backgrounds of her books.

The Artist

FRANK ALOISE left a career as TV artist in 1961 to devote himself exclusively to children's book illustrations. Trained at the Art Students League and the Workshop School of Art, New York, Mr. Aloise has found time to hold a number of exhibits and to engage in volunteer work with blind children at the Light House, New York City. He has illustrated a number of books for Putnam's including a See and Read biography of George Washington.